I0892424

ISSUES TODAY

How Has the #MeToo Movement Changed Society?

Brynn Reinkens

ReferencePoint Press

San Diego, CA

ReferencePoint Press®

© 2021 ReferencePoint Press, Inc.
Printed in the United States

For more information, contact:
ReferencePoint Press, Inc.
PO Box 27779
San Diego, CA 92198
www.ReferencePointPress.com

ALL RIGHTS RESERVED.
No part of this work covered by the copyright hereon may be reproduced or used in any form or by any means—graphic, electronic, or mechanical, including photocopying, recording, taping, web distribution, or information storage retrieval systems—without the written permission of the publisher.

LIBRARY OF CONGRESS CATALOGING-IN-PUBLICATION DATA

Names: Reinkens, Brynn, author.
Title: How has the #MeToo movement changed society? / by Brynn Reinkens.
Description: San Diego, CA : ReferencePoint Press, [2021] | Series: Issues today | Includes bibliographical references and index.
Identifiers: LCCN 2020002089 (print) | LCCN 2020002090 (ebook) | ISBN 9781682828892 (library binding) | ISBN 9781682828908 (ebook)
Subjects: LCSH: Sexual abuse victims--United States. | Sexual harassment--United States. | Sex discrimination--United States. | Responsibility--United States.
Classification: LCC HV6592 .R45 2021 (print) | LCC HV6592 (ebook) | DDC 362.8830973--dc23
LC record available at https://lccn.loc.gov/2020002089
LC ebook record available at https://lccn.loc.gov/2020002090

CONTENTS

Breaking the Silence

In 2019, three former Fox News hosts founded an organization whose goal is to prevent businesses from hiding cases of sexual harassment and discrimination. The organization, called Lift Our Voices, seeks to promote workplace equality for women as well as business environments free from fear of retaliation for those who speak up. Lift Our Voices is one of the many outgrowths of the #MeToo Movement. The movement became a catalyst for social change in 2017 when the hashtag went viral online. These two little words—*me too*—illuminated the magnitude of sexual harassment and assault experienced by women from all walks of life. The millions of women who posted the hashtag online demonstrated that sexual misconduct was prevalent and needed to be addressed. One of the biggest revelations of the #MeToo Movement was how businesses of all sorts were using the law to silence those who had experienced workplace sexual harassment.

In many companies, a mandatory arbitration clause is included in the large stack of papers new employees must sign. A mandatory arbitration clause is a legally binding contract that prevents a workplace conflict from going to court. By 2017 more than half of all American workers had signed away their right to sue their employer for sexual harassment and gender or racial discrimination, according to a study by the nonpartisan think tank the Economic Policy Institute. Instead, sexual harassment suits and other workplace disputes are settled out of court. Settlement agreements usually offer large sums of money to an employee who accuses a coworker or supervisor of misconduct. In exchange, that employee must sign a nondisclosure agreement (NDA). An NDA is a contract by which the employee agrees to not disclose confidential information, such as the details of sexual harassment in the company.

Prohibited from Speaking Out

The three women who founded Lift Our Voices had complained about workplace sexual harassment by Fox chief executive officer (CEO) Roger Ailes. The three women—Gretchen Carlson, Julie Roginsky and Diana Falzon—had all settled their claims against Ailes. But those settlements carried a high price. All three had been required to sign mandatory arbitration clauses and NDAs. This meant they could not seek justice in a court of law nor could they speak publicly about the sexual misconduct they had experienced at work.

> **"'Winning' my complaint with a settlement and a nondisclosure agreement meant I was, essentially, forced into silence."[1]**
>
> —Gretchen Carlson, former Fox News host and cofounder of Lift Our Voices

The Lift Our Voices founders say that NDAs are used to silence those who speak against sexual misconduct while simultaneously protecting those in positions of power. If someone breaks their NDA after a settlement has been reached—for example, by publicly giving the details about how they were sexually harassed at work—then they face the risk of being sued by their employer. "'Winning' my complaint with a settlement and a nondisclosure agreement meant I was, essentially, forced into silence,"[1] says Carlson.

Although none of the three women has made public the details of her interactions with Ailes, they all have been vocal in their calls for an end to sexual misconduct and gender discrimination at Fox. They believe their calls for change have hurt their careers. Carlson has said that she was let go from the network after she refused Ailes's sexual advances and complained about the severe culture of harassment at the network. Similarly, Roginsky claims to have been blacklisted by most major networks after she reached her settlement with Ailes. A blacklist refers to a list of people or

Allegations of sexual harassment against Fox CEO Roger Ailes (pictured) led to the founding of Lift Our Voices, an organization that strives to shine a light on workplace sexual harassment and discrimination.

things that are regarded as unacceptable or untrustworthy and should be excluded or avoided. Roginsky says she has been unable to find comparable work since she left Fox, and she blames that on her tainted reputation. "Networks don't want to work with us because they're afraid that we'll call out bad behavior, like we called out bad behavior at Fox,"[2] Roginsky says.

Though the #MeToo Movement has put the spotlight on how prevalent sexual misconduct is, there is much more work to be done in creating safer places for women. In the years since #MeToo went viral, activist organizations like Lift Our Voices are now going the extra mile in advocating for justice for those who are subjected to sexual harassment.

The Role of the #MeToo Movement

The biggest change that has occurred in the years since #MeToo is a new culture of accountability. When someone is accused of sexual misconduct, the accuser is to be believed, not ignored nor blamed as had been common in years prior. This has led to hundreds of men resigning from their jobs after being accused of sexual misconduct. The movement has created popular demand for new laws as well as new politicians to implement them. Many of these laws pertain to businesses. For example, many states have passed laws that limit or even forbid the use of NDAs in corporate sexual harassment disputes.

Change can be felt in many industries. In 2018, for example, twenty thousand Google employees went on strike to force changes in how the company resolves sexual misconduct disputes. Women in the entertainment industry and Hollywood have created organizations like Time's Up to help women who do not have access to legal resources or funds to still be able to hold their harassers accountable. In the financial industry, Wells Fargo became the first major bank to formally abolish the use of NDAs. The #MeToo influence has even reached into education. In many schools and universities, teachers and professors are now required to include lessons on sexual harassment and consent.

But as with all major changes, reluctance, uncertainty, and unintended consequences emerge. In the workplace, many fear false accusations. Others are concerned that they will be punished for an act that they did not even know was perceived as harassment. In some cases, this has manifested as women being excluded from workplace interactions or jobs. But this does not portray a grim future for women. Now more than ever, women are empowered to speak up against injustices made against them. The #MeToo Movement has created a network of safety that encourages people to say that they have had enough and demand justice for the injustices they have faced.

Solidarity, Awareness, and Accountability

In the fall of 2017, the *New York Times* published Jodi Kantor and Megan Twohey's investigative article alleging that film producer and Hollywood mogul Harvey Weinstein had engaged in sexual misconduct—ranging from harassment to rape—for more than three decades. Several of the women interviewed told a narrative that closely mirrored the experience lived by actress Ashley Judd. Judd explained that in 1996, when her acting career was just taking off, she was invited by Weinstein to a business breakfast meeting at an upscale hotel. Knowing that the right conversation with this man could directly result in scripts, roles, magazine coverage, and influence, she gladly agreed. To her surprise, upon her arrival, Judd was escorted to his suite instead of to the hotel's restaurant. As the door to the suite opened, it became apparent that Weinstein had not invited her there to discuss her career. She said he was dressed in a bathrobe, offered to give her a massage, tried to elicit help in picking out his clothing, and urged her to watch him take a shower. He persisted in his unwanted advances despite her many refusals.

The Whisper Network

As it turns out, Judd was not the only woman to experience this sort of treatment from Weinstein. In the weeks, months, and even years after the publication of the *New York Times* article, it became clear that about fifty young women had been similarly abused. Though the *New York Times* report initiated public awareness of

Weinstein's behavior, a secret "whisper network" had circulated in and around Hollywood for years. Women at all levels of the entertainment industry had been quietly talking to each other about their experiences with Weinstein. Many had also been gathering evidence in the form of legal records, e-mails, and internal records from the companies run by Weinstein: Miramax and the Weinstein Company.

Most of those who claimed to have experienced Weinstein's predatory sexual behavior were prohibited from speaking about it. Many had been persuaded to accept payouts. In doing so,

Early in her acting career, Ashley Judd (pictured) was invited to a business breakfast with Hollywood film producer Harvey Weinstein. Shortly after arriving it became clear to her that Weinstein had something altogether different in mind.

they signed NDAs that legally required them to maintain a strict code of confidentiality regarding both the agreements and the events that led to them. Furthermore, speaking out could be very costly because association with this powerful company head could make or break one's career, reputation, and future prosperity. When combined with the overbearing power dynamic, many women feared that had they spoken up, they would not have been believed anyway. Likewise, the women who did speak up in, and after, the publication of the *New York Times* article did so at great risk to their careers and well-being.

In the months and years prior to Kantor and Twohey's article, the *New York Times* had committed to investigating and reporting on sexual harassment stories. These ranged from other harassment claims against media moguls like Roger Ailes to top executives in Silicon Valley. "I know it seems like those were many sexual harassment stories ago, but at the time, they were really a light-bulb moment for the paper because they made us realize there may be a lot more buried truths here,"[3] says Kantor. While many people in the industry had heard stories of Weinstein's behavior, almost no one knew the extent of his misconduct. Most women who told their stories to the *New York Times* had never met one another, let alone heard of their shared experiences. Among them were Ambra Battilana, Rose McGowan, and Zelda Perkins, all of whom reached financial settlements tied to their agreement to remain silent.

A Viral Hashtag

Massive media coverage followed the initial *New York Times* article. Suddenly, dozens of other women were quoted in additional articles detailing similar experiences with Weinstein. Readers, and especially the Hollywood community, were disgusted and outraged at the magnitude of such behavior. One of them was actress Alyssa Milano, herself a survivor of sexual assault.

On October 15, 2017, Milano received this message from a friend. It read, "Suggested by a friend: if all the women who have been sexually harassed or assaulted wrote 'me too' as a status,

Tarana Burke's Vision for the #MeToo Movement

As the #MeToo Movement has grown in scale, it also has collided with forces of backlash and misinterpretation. In 2018 one of the movement's founders, Tarana Burke, described her vision of the movement and its focus:

> This is a movement about the 1 in 4 girls and 1 in 6 boys who are sexually assaulted every year and carry those wounds into adulthood. It's about the 84% of trans women who will be sexually assaulted this year. And the indigenous women who are three-and-a-half times more likely to be sexually assaulted than any other group. Or people with disabilities who are 7 times more likely to [be] sexually abused. It's about the 60% of black girls like me who will be experiencing sexual assault before they turn 18. . . . This is a movement about the far-reaching power of empathy. And so it's about the millions and millions of people who one year ago raised their hands to say Me Too. . . .
>
> My vision for the Me Too Movement is part of a collective vison to see a world free of sexual violence and I believe we can build that world. . . . But in order to get there . . . we have to dismantle the building blocks of sexual violence: Power and Privilege. We must recognize that anybody in a position of power comes with privilege, and this renders those without power more vulnerable. But we reshape that imbalance by speaking out against it in unison.

Tarana Burke, "Me Too Is a Movement, Not a Moment." TEDWomen 2018. www.ted.com.

we might give people a sense of the magnitude of the problem." [4] Milano liked this idea, but she wanted to do more than just highlight the extent of the problem. She wanted to use the media attention to redirect the focus off of the men and onto the personal stories of victims and survivors. Prior to sharing her tweet, Milano added her own additional sentence: "If you've been sexually harassed or assaulted write 'me too' as a reply to this tweet."[5] This called on her Twitter followers to retweet her post as well as share their own #MeToo stories.

Overnight, she received roughly fifty-five thousand individual replies. By the next night, her tweet had been transformed into the number-one-trending hashtag on Twitter, reaching far beyond the boundaries of the United States and even the English language.

As the hashtag grew in strength and numbers, Milano and women around the world began to feel a subtle but definite sense of empowerment and community. She started a trend that gave survivors a voice and created a worldwide awareness of a problem that had for too long been ignored. Milano initially got credit for starting what came to be known as the #MeToo Movement, but it turns out that this movement had been around for over a decade.

Earlier Origins

It originally began in 2006 thanks to social justice advocate Tarana Burke. Burke had devoted her entire career to advocating for minority women who were survivors of sexual violence. She began the movement as a platform for helping women of color who experience sexual abuse. "Frustrated by all the sexual violence I saw in

Long before #MeToo went viral on Twitter, social justice advocate Tarana Burke (pictured) began using the words Me Too *to show solidarity and to support the women of color who experience sexual violence.*

my community, I pulled out a piece of paper and I wrote 'Me Too' on the top of it," she recalled in her 2018 TED talk. "And I proceeded to write out an action plan for building a movement based on empathy between survivors that would help us feel like we could heal."[6]

Burke transformed her action plan into a MySpace page that provided a network for survivors of sexual violence. It allowed them to speak truthfully about their experiences and shared access to available resources. "There was no such thing as viral back then. But if there was this would be as close to that as possible,"[7] says Burke. The response was bigger than anything she or her colleagues had ever imagined.

When Burke and those familiar with her work first saw Milano's #MeToo trending on Twitter, they feared that overnight Burke's hard work would be overshadowed by the celebrity of famous white women. Having long worked on raising awareness about sexual violence experienced by people of color, those who were acquainted with Burke's social advocacy began to speak out. They illuminated the fact that "Me Too" was close to the heart of survivors of sexual violence and that Burke was the movement's originator. Once aware of the phrase's origins, Milano publicly apologized to Burke, and the two women joined forces. Together, they propelled the movement forward.

The Women Who Spoke Up

In the year following Milano's October 2017 tweet, the hashtag *#MeToo* had been used over 19 million times on Twitter—and by users from countries around the world. Celebrity and influencer responses to the hashtag began to dominate the media. Big-name celebrities, including Lady Gaga, Viola Davis, and Taylor Swift, came forward detailing their own experiences with being subjected to sexual misconduct. And unlike so many women before them, they began naming the perpetrators. Men who had held positions of influence in all sectors of society were being called out for behavior that had been occurring, in some cases, for years. These high-profile stories lent credibility to voices from all sectors of society. "When multiple harassment claims bring down a charmer like former *Today* show host Matt Lauer, women who thought they had no recourse see a new, wide-open door. When a movie star says #MeToo, it becomes easier to believe the cook who's been quietly enduring for years,"[8] *Time* magazine reporters wrote in 2017.

The movement continued to grow as more women—and not just those in the entertainment industry—responded with stories of their own. The stories spanned the spectrum of employment, race, gender, class, and sexual orientation. "#MeToo—I have been fired from jobs for not sleeping with the boss, fired for not letting customers grab me . . . It sucks thinking about this stuff,"[9] tweeted one of Milano's early responders, Amanda Yennie, who had worked as a restaurant hostess. Another woman, Nora Young, wrote, "A college prof once told me 'boys will be boys' when a classmate sexually assaulted me."[10]

"The collective pain we've felt has turned into collective power. It's amazing."[11]

—Alyssa Milano, the actress who helped #MeToo go viral

#MeToo was no ordinary viral hashtag. It demonstrated the strength of numbers. "The collective pain we've felt has turned into collective power. It's amazing,"[11] said Milano. Though thrilled with the movement's success, Burke had concerns. She worried that the media would direct most of its attention to white celebrities and high-profile figures rather than to ordinary people, particularly women of color, who are statistically twice as likely to be victims of sexual assault as their white counterparts. "Women of color, transwomen, queer people—our stories get pushed aside and our pain is never prioritized,"[12] said Burke.

"Women of color, transwomen, queer people—our stories get pushed aside and our pain is never prioritized."[12]

—Tarana Burke, social activist and founder of the #MeToo Movement

She continues to redirect the movement's focus back toward mem-

Protesters in San Francisco demanded change as the #MeToo Movement spread beyond the entertainment industry to other segments of society.

bers of society who are harassed because of their gender identity, economic powerlessness, or skin color. Burke states that the number one thing she hears from people is that the #MeToo Movement has forgotten black, Hispanic, and Native American women. "Every day, we hear some version of that. But this is what I'm here to tell you," she said in her 2018 keynote address at the Facing Race conference in Detroit. "The #MeToo movement is not defined by what the media has told you. We are the movement, and so I need you to not opt out of the #MeToo movement. I need you to reframe your [racial justice] work to include sexual violence. That's how we take back the narrative. Stop giving your power away to white folks."[13]

Finding Solidarity in Numbers

Solidarity across all walks of life harnessed the power of the #MeToo Movement. The culture was changed by working in unison. Because the movement does not have a single leader, *Time* magazine named "the Silence Breakers" as its 2017 Person of the Year. This refers to the dozens of women interviewed by *Time* to represent the millions of women from all segments of society who said, "Me Too." The hashtag provided "an umbrella of solidarity for millions of people to come forward and share their stories,"[14] explains *Time*. The women featured in the article represented a diverse group. Celebrities like Judd, Swift, and Milano were shown beside a strawberry picker, an engineer, a corporate lobbyist, a hospital worker, and others. Although they had different backgrounds—different socioeconomic status, ages, religions, and family lives—they shared one unifying characteristic: all had been subjected to some sort of sexual misconduct. These newly empowered voices reject the inappropriate, violating, and sometimes criminal misconduct they experienced. This has begun to erode tolerance for silence; a new normal of condemnation has taken hold.

Time found that most of the women they interviewed had experienced sexual misconduct not just once but multiple times. Many described the feeling that they were somehow at fault and struggled to identify which of their actions might have been to blame for their treatment. "I kept thinking, did I do something, did I say something, did I look a certain way to make him think that was O.K.?,"[15] reported the anonymous hospital worker. There had also been immense fear of what would happen to them if they spoke out publicly about their situations.

One of those interviewed by *Time* was Taylor Swift. The hugely popular singer was included in the article because of the powerful and symbolic way she faced her sexual harasser. After Swift reported an incident in which radio personality David Mueller had reached under her skirt as they posed for a photo together, Mueller was fired. He, in turn, sued Swift for millions of dollars in damages; in response, she countersued for only one

"I kept thinking, did I do something, did I say something, did I look a certain way to make him think that was O.K.?"[15]

—An anonymous hospital worker

dollar. Swift reasoned that if he was "brazen enough to assault me under these risky circumstances, imagine what he might do to a vulnerable, young artist if given the chance."[16] Empowered stances like the one taken by Swift against her harasser have led to hundreds of men being fired or resigning from their positions.

The Downfall of the Powerful and Privileged

In the eighteen months after the initial *New York Times* article about Harvey Weinstein, public allegations of sexual misconduct were brought against more than 250 esteemed and powerful men. Many of these men were later stripped of their awards, dismissed from their jobs, forced to endure sullied reputations, and, in some cases, were charged with crimes. Weinstein, for instance, was fired from the company he cofounded and was pressured to resign from his seat on its board of directors. He was removed from the Academy of Motion Picture Arts and Sciences. His criminal trial for charges of predatory sexual assault, criminal sexual act, and first-degree and third-degree rape began in January 2020 in New York. He pleaded not guilty to all of these charges and insists that all sexual encounters have been consensual. More than forty women have publicly spoken of their experiences with Weinstein, but only six testified at the trial. At the close of arguments, Weinstein was found guilty on two counts: criminal sexual assault in the first degree and rape in the third degree. He was acquitted on two counts of predatory sexual assault. He was sentenced to twenty-three years in prison. His trial on similar charges in a Los Angeles case was pending as of March 2020.

The rapid erosion of the culture of silence and tolerance that protected powerful men has been dubbed "the Weinstein effect." This is a trend that mirrors Weinstein's case as sexual misconduct allegations continue to be made against high-profile men. Among those called out during this period—who experienced loss of livelihood, wealth, assets, relationships, credibility, respectability, and more—were comedians Aziz Ansari and Louis C.K.; actors Kevin Spacey, Morgan Freeman, Richard Dreyfuss, and Ben Affleck;

Allegations Against President Trump

More than twenty women have publicly accused President Donald Trump of sexual misconduct. One of these women, Rachel Crooks, gave her story to the *Washington Post*. In this February 2018 article, she describes the 2006 encounter:

> It all happened at Trump Tower. I had just moved to New York City, and I was working as a secretary for another company in the building. That's where he forced himself on me. . . . He started kissing me on one cheek and then the other cheek. He was talking to me in-between kisses, asking me where I was from, or if I wanted to be a model. He wouldn't let go of my hand, and then he went right in and started kissing me on the lips. . . . It felt like a long kiss. . . . The whole thing probably lasted two minutes, maybe less.

On February 20, 2018, Trump denied Crooks's account, responding with this tweet:

> A woman I don't know and, to the best of my knowledge, never met, is on the FRONT PAGE of the Fake News Washington Post saying I kissed her (for two minutes yet) in the lobby of Trump Tower 12 years ago. Never happened! Who would do this in a public space with live security . . . cameras running. Another False Accusation. Why doesn't @washingtonpost report the story of the women taking money to make up stories about me? One had her home mortgage paid off.

Quoted in Eli Saslow, "Is Any One Listening," *Washington Post*, February 19, 2018. www.washingtonpost.com.

Quoted in Anne North, "This Trump Accusers Story Is Well-Supported and Convincing. His Response Is Not," Vox, February 20, 2018. www.vox.com.

illusionist David Copperfield; political commentator Bill O'Reilly; and rappers Nelly and R. Kelly. A movement that caught fire in Hollywood soon spread to men in positions of power across all industries. Allegations of sexual harassment were leveled against three Google executives. The senior vice president of mobile and digital content, Andy Rubin, was accused of coercing a female employee into oral sex in 2013. Alphabet (Google's parent company) executive Richard DeVaul reportedly asked a job candidate to remove her shirt and offered her a back rub during her interview in 2018. Three employees alleged that Google's vice president, Amit Singhal, had groped a coworker in 2016. All three men were fired.

Many politicians have been accused of sexual misconduct as well. At least nine elected officials have resigned from their positions after being publicly accused of improper behavior, ranging from harassment to assault. Many others, the most notable of which are President Donald Trump and Supreme Court justice Brett Kavanaugh, have successfully fought against allegations of sexual improprieties. Nonetheless, they too have felt the collective power that has created not only a shift in mainstream culture but also has altered the national and international political and legal landscape.

An Altered Legal and Political Landscape

The #MeToo Movement has led to changes in US laws and policies. New laws have been made and new faces can now be seen making those laws. "We have seen laws passed in several states that strengthen protections against harassment. I would be surprised if any of these laws passed, or were even introduced, in the absence of the #MeToo Movement,"[17] says Emily Martin, the vice president of the National Women's Law Center.

New Laws, New Protections

Many states have adopted changes to their legal codes in efforts to respond to concerns aired by the #MeToo Movement. Some states, such as California, have banned nondisclosure and other confidentiality agreements as a condition of employment or as part of settlement agreements. Other states, such as Washington and Connecticut, require companies with more than fifty employees to report the number of sexual harassment claims they have settled. Dozens of states have also expanded sexual harassment training requirements that companies must adhere to, and now all of the

> "We have seen laws passed in several states that strengthen protections against harassment. I would be surprised if any of these laws passed, or were even introduced, in the absence of the #MeToo movement."[17]
>
> —Emily Martin, National Women's Law Center

nation's publicly traded companies are required to include at least one woman on their boards.

Some of the strongest new protections include laws limiting or banning NDAs. A big motivator behind these new legal codes was the fact that Harvey Weinstein and his companies had at least seventy NDAs with women who had lodged sexual assault allegations against him. This proved to lawmakers that NDAs could be used as a barrier to women who seek justice for sexual misconduct in the workplace. Since 2017, thirteen states have changed or enacted legislation regarding NDAs. The laws differ by state. In Arizona, for instance, an individual is entitled to break the NDA if asked about criminal sex offenses by law enforcement. Illinois has rendered void any contractual clause that, as a condition of employment, prohibits the disclosure of workplace sexual discrimination or harassment. Several states and some cities have banned the use of NDAs in settlement agreements, and others have placed limits on the use of NDAs in these agreements. Vermont, Illinois, Maryland, and New York City have passed laws that require companies to file reports on internal investigations resulting from sexual harassment

A young woman accepts a job offer. In some states, nondisclosure and other confidentiality agreements are no longer a condition of employment.

claims that have been resolved through settlements. This has been done to remedy the lack of transparency and accountability that hinders potential reform. Finally, Illinois, Maryland, New Jersey, New York, Vermont, and Washington have prohibited employers from compelling their employees to waive their right to go to court in instances regarding sexual harassment or discrimination.

Another course of action that states have undertaken in the wake of #MeToo is extending statutes of limitations. Statutes of limitations are laws that set the maximum time a party may have to take legal action. If this window of time is relatively short, it can act as a barrier to accessing justice, especially for survivors who are also coping with varying degrees of trauma. For this reason, states are beginning to lengthen this period of time in sexual misconduct cases.

They are also adopting laws aimed at prevention. In 2018, several states passed laws aimed at strengthening preventive measures in the workplace. These laws have required the creation of sexual harassment training programs and have made them mandatory for many businesses.

Women Make Political History

The #MeToo Movement has inspired more than new laws. It has also inspired new people to seek office as lawmakers. In 2018 a record number of women ran for public office at all levels of government. They ran for many reasons. For some, the election of Donald Trump as president created a sense of urgency to bring more women's voices into the federal government. Others felt energized and emboldened by the women's marches—the worldwide protests that took place the day after Trump's inauguration. These marches occurred because many believed Trump's behavior to be anti-woman. Anger was another motivating factor, and many ran for office in response to the revelations brought to light by the #MeToo Movement. "A lot of us women thought that by taking nontraditional jobs, or working really hard in our careers, we were making the world a better place," said Mikie Sherrill during her 2018 election campaign to become a US representative from New Jersey. "And yet we realized when we saw the attacks on women, and how women's voices are silenced when they're talking about sexual violence, we need to do more. We need to have a seat at the table legislatively."[18]

"We realized when we saw the attacks on women, and how women's voices are silenced when they're talking about sexual violence, we need to do more. We need to have a seat at the table legislatively."[18]

—Mikie Sherrill, member of the US House of Representatives

Sherrill was one of 117 women who won elections in 2018. Thirty-five women were elected to the US House of Representatives. The 435-member House now has 102 female members, more than the previous high of 84 in 1992. Thirteen women were elected to the Senate, which increased the total number of female senators from twelve to twenty-five. At age twenty-nine, Alexandria Ocasio-Cortez, a Latina from New York, became the youngest

Among the thirty-five women elected to the US House of Representatives in 2018, is New Yorker Alexandria Ocasio-Cortez (pictured). At age twenty-nine, she became the youngest female member of the House.

Time to Act

On May 9, 2019, Anita Hill, the law professor who accused Supreme Court nominee Clarence Thomas of sexual harassment, wrote an opinion piece that appeared in the *New York Times*. In it, she argued that had the government taken sexual misconduct seriously during Thomas's hearing in 1991, women may have felt empowered to speak up at that time:

> If [in 1991] the Senate Judiciary Committee, led then by Mr. [Joe] Biden, had done its job and held a hearing that showed that its members understood the seriousness of sexual harassment and other forms of sexual violence, the cultural shift we saw in 2017 after #MeToo might have begun in 1991—with the support of the government.
>
> If the government had shown that it would treat survivors with dignity and listen to women, it could have had a ripple effect. People agitating for change would have been operating from a position of strength. It could have given institutions . . . greater license to take more decisive action to end the scourge of harassment. And research shows that if leaders convey that they won't tolerate harassment, people within an organization typically obey. . . .
>
> Survivors and their supporters need acknowledgment and justice. Words of condolence can never substitute for action aimed at ending the harm. There are measures that would show that our government is ready to respond to survivors.

Anita Hill, "Anita Hill: Let's Talk About How to End Sexual Violence," *New York Times*, May 9, 2019. www.nytimes.com.

female member of the House of Representatives. In New Mexico, Debra Haaland became one of the first Native American women to serve in Congress. Michigan's Rashida Tlaib and Minnesota's Ilhan Omar won their House races, making them the first Muslim women elected to Congress. In Tennessee, Marsha Blackburn became that state's first female US senator. Other women elected to legislative seats in 2018 included Ayanna Pressley, who became the first black woman to represent Massachusetts in the House; Faith Winter, who was elected to the Colorado Senate; and Katie Muth, who was elected to the Pennsylvania Senate.

The Topic of Debate: Sexual Misconduct

Many women were elected to federal, state, or local office because of how they addressed the issue of sexual misconduct during their campaigns. Pressley talked publicly about her experiences with rape and childhood sexual abuse. Winter and Muth called on fellow Democratic incumbents accused of sexual misconduct to step down. Anna Eskamani, who won a position in the Florida House of Representatives, spoke openly about her workplace sexual harassment experiences. "This last year we saw an undeniable shift in how we tolerate sexual harassment and how we talk about it," Eskamani said during her campaign. By opening up about her own experiences with sexual misconduct, she said, "[I began] to understand how my personal experiences had huge political implications—that the personal is political in that way."[19]

The issues raised by these women while running for office were some of the same issues that inspired many of them to run in the first place. Among the issues cited were Trump's election as president, the confirmation hearing of Supreme Court justice Brett Kavanaugh, and the many shades of discontent expressed by the explosion of the #MeToo Movement. "These lived experiences fueled my decision to run for office and serve as my own moral compass," says Eskamani. "The 2016 election inspired me to run for office, but it was the Women's March in 2017 that further solidified my aspirations to do this work, and it was the #MeToo Movement that reminded me that it's so important that we not only run but that we win."[20]

> **"It was the #MeToo Movement that reminded me that it's so important that we not only run but that we win."[20]**
>
> —Anna Eskamani, member of the Florida House of Representatives

The #MeToo Movement was not only a crucial topic for electoral candidates but also for voters. A 2018 survey conducted by the Barbara Lee Family Foundation, a nonprofit organization whose focus is gender equality, revealed that a candidate's stance on sexual misconduct weighed heavily on voters' decisions. Fifty-two percent of respondents said that they would never vote for someone who had been accused of sexual harassment, and 51 percent reported that they would not vote for someone who failed to prioritize addressing sexual misconduct.

Additionally, female voters in 2018 seemed to find connection with female candidates who they believed would take their concerns seriously. As Julie McClain Downey, the senior director of campaign communications at Emily's List, says, "Seeing all of this play out in a way where suddenly you realize that you're not alone, and you can use your voice and your vote to elect someone who will address these issues and not just sweep them under the rug, is pretty remarkable."[21]

The Supreme Court and Sexual Misconduct

While women have made political history in federal, state and local branches of government, progress toward the goals of the #MeToo Movement has taken a different path in the judicial branch, and, more specifically, in the US Supreme Court. The Supreme Court is one of America's most tradition-bound institutions of government. This is because unlike in the executive and legislative branches, Supreme Court justices are not voted into office by the American people directly. Rather, they are nominated by the president, confirmed by the Senate, and, once confirmed, hold office for life. But the judiciary is not immune to the changes taking place in society. It too has changed in the wake of #MeToo.

In the summer of 2018, Supreme Court justice Anthony Kennedy retired and Trump nominated Kavanaugh, a judge on the US Court of Appeals for the District of Columbia, to fill Kennedy's vacant seat. During the nomination process, Christine Blasey Ford, a professor of psychology at Palo Alto University, accused Kavanaugh of sexually assaulting her when they were both high school students. Because the alleged assault occurred in the early 1980s, there was no hard evidence that the Senate Judiciary Committee could rely on, nor were there witnesses other

An allegation of sexual assault dominated the Senate confirmation hearing for US Supreme Court justice nominee Brett Kavanaugh. Kavanaugh, who was eventually confirmed, poses with President Donald Trump after being sworn in.

than Ford and Kavanaugh who could give testimony.

Kavanaugh's confirmation hearing was reminiscent of the confirmation hearing of Clarence Thomas in 1991. Upon nomination to the Supreme Court, both men were confronted with sexual misconduct allegations and were investigated by the Senate Judiciary Committee. In both instances, the Supreme Court nominees strongly rejected the claims made against them as false, but what occurred within the courtrooms of each hearing demonstrate the extent of change that the #MeToo Movement has had in how sexual misconduct is handled within the US government itself.

Presidential Candidates and NDAs

On December 18, 2019, Lift Our Voices, the organization that opposes the use of NDAs in the workplace, sent a letter to all presidential candidates asking them to publicly condemn these agreements. The group's intention was to force discussion of the issue during the 2020 election, particularly in presidential debates. The letter states,

> These NDAs are a driving force in silencing workers and promulgating a culture where employers are able to cover up toxicity, including issues of sexual harassment and gender discrimination, rather than address it and end it. It is time for our leaders to demonstrate that they are on the side of the women and men who have been silenced for too long from discussing the hostility they have encountered by speaking out loudly and publicly against NDAs.

Later, in an interview, Gretchen Carlson (one of the group's founders) stated, "This is incredibly important for a presidential candidate to get on board with. . . . Whether it's the president of the United States, or a person running a company, the buck stops with that person. And they can shift the discussion."

Quoted in Nick Corasaniti, "2020 Candidates Are Asked to Condemn Nondisclosure Agreements," *New York Times*, December 18, 2019. www.nytimes.com.

During Thomas's confirmation hearing, Anita Hill, a law professor at the University of Oklahoma, accused Thomas of sexual harassment in the workplace when they had worked together years earlier. Much like Kavanaugh's hearing, there was no hard evidence, and the Senate members conducting the confirmation hearing could only rely on the testimony of Thomas and Hill.

Prior to Hill's testimony, the hearing rooms of the US Senate had never before heard allegations of sexual misconduct during the process of determining the worthiness of a nominated Supreme Court justice. Hill sat before an all-male panel of senators who grilled her over and over again about the details of her time working for Thomas. The senators questioned her credibility and asked why she had not come forward earlier—questions that in today's #MeToo climate would be labeled as victim blaming.

Moreover, sexual harassment was so normalized and underreported as a problem that many of the senators did not even deem blameworthy the behavior that formed the heart of her allegations.

Twenty-five years later, following a decade of gender equality activism and the #MeToo Movement, the Senate Judiciary Committee conducted a different kind of hearing. The committee hired Rachel Mitchel, an Arizona attorney who specializes in prosecuting sex crimes, to question Ford. The committee's goal was to avoid the earlier scenario in which an all-male group of senators grills the lone female accuser. Though this may seem like a small change, it was actually viewed by many as an acknowledgment of the seriousness of sexual assault. The questioning of Ford by the prosecutor, and by many of the senators, was mostly respectful. During testimony, Ford described how Kavanaugh and his friend drunkenly pushed her into a bedroom during a party, held her down, tried to remove her clothing, and covered her mouth to muffle her screams. She was not asked the humiliating and off-topic questions that Hill had to answer all those years ago. Mitchel, the senators, and the American public greeted Ford's testimony with the empathy that could only arise in an era where it is generally understood that sexual assault is a real and commonly lived experience.

Kavanaugh adamantly denied the allegations made against him. But in his opening statement he also approached sexual misconduct with the seriousness and empathy that the American public demanded. "Allegations of sexual assault must always be taken seriously, always. Those that make allegations always deserve to be heard,"[22] said Kavanaugh. He later went on to say that he believed Ford

"Allegations of sexual assault must always be taken seriously, always. Those that make allegations always deserve to be heard."[22]

—Brett Kavanaugh, nominee to the US Supreme Court

may have experienced some form of sexual assault, but that her accusation that it was him was wholly inaccurate.

Though both Thomas and Kavanaugh were eventually confirmed to the Supreme Court, a massive feminist tide ensued in the years following their confirmations. *Time* named 1992 "the Year of the Woman" when more women than ever before in US history were voted into public office—that is, until the record-breaking 2018 midterm elections. As the #MeToo Movement is ending a culture of normalized sexual harassment, American politics and laws are rapidly following suit and adjusting to this higher standard of respect for and belief of accusers.

The Business World Adapts

The activism behind the #MeToo Movement has done more than just change America's political and legal landscape. Legislators are not the only ones who have heard and responded to altered attitudes about sexual conduct. Businesses of all sorts have embraced this cultural shift, with many companies implementing new measures of their own. This can be seen in institutions ranging from media and entertainment to Silicon Valley and Wall Street.

The Entertainment Industry

While job dismissals and trials are the clearest evidence of changed attitudes, the entertainment industry has taken steps to level the scales of gender and power dynamics. In 2018 a national organization of female farmworkers wrote a letter of solidarity to the Hollywood women involved in the Weinstein scandal. "Dear sisters," the letter began, "Even though we work in very different environments, we share a common experience of being preyed upon by individuals who have the power to hire, fire, blacklist and otherwise threaten our economic, physical and emotional security."[23] The farmworkers organization had been working against workplace sexual harassment for decades, and the sincerity of the letter inspired these Hollywood celebrities to work with them. Together, they

> **"Even though we work in very different environments, we share a common experience of being preyed upon by individuals who have the power to hire, fire, blacklist and otherwise threaten our economic, physical and emotional security."[23]**
>
> —A national organization of female farmworkers

created an organization called Time's Up. Time's Up was formed to work toward gender equity and take action to eliminate sexual misconduct in all areas of modern life. For example, Time's Up spoke at the shareholder meeting of Google's parent company, Alphabet, and urged them to release their median pay data for race and gender. Time's Up says, "Google has refused to release data on the median gender and racial pay gap at the company. That's the most important piece of information to assess whether women are paid fairly and given equal opportunities to advance."[24]

At the core of Time's Up is the Time's Up Legal Defense Fund (LDF), which has raised more than $22 million. The money is being used to connect survivors of workplace sexual harassment and retaliation from all industries with lawyers and other resources to assist in seeking justice. The fund has received immense support and donations from leaders in the film and entertainment industry as well as smaller donations from individuals and communities from all over the world. In 2018 alone, the Time's Up LDF responded to more than thirty-seven hundred workers from

After harvesting raspberries, a young farmworker sorts and packages them. An organization that represents farmworkers joined with Hollywood celebrities to form Time's Up.

all fifty states by connecting them to local lawyers. In the first six months of operation, $5 million was allocated for legal services in seventy-five cases of sexual harassment. Approximately eight hundred lawyers have joined the networks created by the fund, and $750,000 has been awarded in outreach grants to eighteen organizations that work with low-income workers.

Further Strides Made by Hollywood

Hollywood made further strides against sexual misconduct in 2018 by adopting the Anti-Sexual Harassment Guidelines developed by the Producers Guild of America (PGA). The PGA worked with Time's Up to create this new set of policies. The guidelines include mandatory anti–sexual harassment training for employees working on all movie and television sets. It also recommends "designating at least two individuals, ideally of different genders, that cast/crew members can approach if they are subject to or witness harassment."[25]

Hollywood has continued to advance the discussion of workplace conduct in other ways. The Hollywood Commission on Eliminating Sexual Harassment and Advancing Equality was created in 2017. It is in the process of developing policies that promote inclusion and diversity and that protect people in the entertainment industry from bias and harassment. Toward that end, in November 2019 the commission launched an industrywide survey of anyone who has worked in or sought employment in any area of entertainment. Survey participants were to answer questions anonymously. The goal was to collect useful data that could then be used to strengthen policies for protecting against sexual harassment. "The sole way to build safe, respectful workplaces that give equal opportunity in the film, television, commercial, music, and theatre industries is to have a clear, data driven and supported understanding of the culture where people work,"[26] a statement from the commission reads.

Not only is the entertainment industry evolving to the advancement of sexual harassment protections, but the culture and

These actresses are among many who wore black at the 2018 Golden Globe Awards ceremony. The black attire was a protest against sexual harassment and an affirmation of the power of the #MeToo Movement.

attitudes of individuals in Hollywood are changing as well. At the 2018 Golden Globe Awards, a ceremony that recognizes excellence in film and television, signs of the #MeToo Movement were everywhere. Most of the celebrities walking the red carpet wore black to protest sexual harassment and raise awareness for Time's Up. When asked by the press at this ceremony why they had dressed in black, nearly every answer was the same: the decision to wear black was intended to call attention to the power of the #MeToo Movement. "It just became clear that

> **"We wanted to stand up and do something for all people to say time's up on discrimination, harassment and abuse in the work place."[27]**
>
> —Reese Witherspoon, actress

with all of the news that's been coming out that it couldn't just be business as normal. We wanted to stand up and do something for all people to say time's up on discrimination, harassment and abuse in the work place,"[27] said actress Reese Witherspoon.

Other Globe attendees, such as actress Debra Messing, used their red carpet moment to elaborate on a broader agenda. Messing called for greater inclusivity and diversity. "I am wearing black to thank and honor all of the brave whistle blowers who came forward, shared their stories of harassment, assault, and discrimination. I'm wearing black to stand in solidarity with my sisters all over the globe and I'm here to celebrate the rollout of this incredible initiative Time's Up. We want diversity, we want intersectional gender parity, equal pay,"[28] Messing said. Here, Messing was referring to the complex way different forms of discrimination overlap, how racial and gender discrimination are intertwined and reinforce each other, and how in order to resolve one form of discrimination, the other must be remediated as well. Those wearing black at the Golden Globes were not alone in their symbolic statement. People from all walks of life and throughout all industries watched in solidarity with the onscreen stars as they recognized the power #MeToo had in not only ending sexual harassment in many industries but in creating a larger push for gender equality as well.

"I'm here to celebrate the rollout of this incredible initiative Time's Up. We want diversity, we want intersectional gender parity, equal pay."[28]

—Debra Messing, actress

The Technology Sector

Originally the #MeToo movement was focused on the entertainment industry. Subsequently, massive media attention rippled into national politics and state legislatures as they implemented new legal requirements for companies. But as time goes on, these ripples have turned into waves, and now companies across a wide spectrum of industries are being forced to act.

VIEWPOINT

Gender Inequality Could Hurt the Economy

In a *Harvard Business Review* article, business innovator and author Nilofer Merchant discusses how sexual harassment leads to women leaving their jobs and creates a male-dominated workforce. This, she argues, restricts the potential for contributions made by women and, in turn, harms the economy:

> Up to 85% of women report that they have been sexually harassed at work, according to a 2016 report by the Equal Employment Opportunity Commission. . . . These women say things like: "I quit" or "I left that place," Or "maybe I shouldn't be in [this industry].". . .
>
> As people drop out, opt out, and tune out of their chosen fields, it affects the whole economy. . . .
>
> The development of new ideas is what allows economies to grow richer year after year. . . . Too often, ideas are considered or dimissed based on *who* contributes them, and how powerful the person—not the ideas themselves—are.
>
> Just as recently as September [2017], *The Economist* reported that "new ideas are getting hard to find.". . .
>
> Those economists seem to think we've run out of ideas, but I'm wondering if it's something else. Could it be that institutionalized patriarchy—the system in which men predominantly hold the power and women are largely excluded from it—is itself . . . slowing economic progress? Could it be that many women's contributions are blocked by those currently in charge? Could it be that women are gaslighted into believing their ideas aren't as worthy? . . . Surely there is an economic impact in all of that.

Nilofer Merchant, "The Insidious Economic Impact of Sexual Harassment," *Harvard Business Review*, November 29, 2017. https://hbr.org.

Silicon Valley and the technology sector have long been riddled with sexism, harassment, and a lack of opportunities for female employees, as has become apparent in the #MeToo era. An investigation launched by the US Department of Labor in 2017 found evidence of pay discrimination throughout the industry, with women generally being paid less than men for the same type

VIEWPOINT

Efforts to Achieve Gender Equality Could Hurt the Economy

In a 2018 speech, political commentator Heather Mac Donald argues that the #MeToo Movement has reignited a push for diversity in America, but the economy will suffer as a result:

> Our nation is about to be transformed, thanks to the #MeToo movement. I am not speaking about a cessation of sexual predation in the workplace. If that were the only consequence of #MeToo, the movement would clearly be a force for good. Unfortunately, its effects are going to be more sweeping and destructive. #MeToo is going to unleash a new torrent of gender and race quotas throughout the economy and culture, on the theory that all disparities in employment and institutional representation are due to harassment and bias. The resulting distortions of decision-making will be largely invisible; we will usually not know of the superior candidates for a job who were passed over in the drive for gender parity. But the net consequence will be a loss of American competitiveness and scientific achievement."

Heather Mac Donald, "The Negative Impact of the #MeToo Movement," Manhattan Institute, May 1, 2018. www.manhattan-institute.org.

of work. That same year, as the #MeToo Movement picked up steam, the industry was faced with a heightened wave of discrimination and sexual harassment scandals.

Susan Fowler, a former software engineer at Uber, published a blog post in February 2017 outlining her allegations of sexual harassment, the company's reluctance to act, and a toxic work culture for female employees. Uber immediately launched an internal investigation. By June, Uber had fired more than twenty employees for alleged harassment, discrimination, and bullying. Among those fired were Jeff Jones, the president and marketing chief; Gautam Gupta, the finance chief; and Emil Michael, the senior vice president. As Uber continued to face widespread criticism from the public and its investors, the company launched its 180 Days of Change, a campaign aimed at reshaping the company's tarnished image. The day after this initiative was launched, CEO and founder Travis Kalanick resigned. Five of the company's investors had requested his resignation. "I love Uber more than anything in the world and at this difficult moment in my personal life I have accepted the investors' request to step aside so that Uber can go back to building rather than be distracted with another fight,"[29] Kalanick said in a statement to the *New York Times*. Many claim that the Uber scandal was the tech industry's #MeToo moment. But changes caused by #MeToo did not stop here for the technology sector; it was really just the beginning.

The Google Walkout

Between 2014 and 2018, three Google executives resigned after sexual misconduct allegations were made against them. But then on October 26, 2018, the *New York Times* published an article describing how Google had given two of these top executives huge pay packages in exchange for their resignations. The article noted that this was done even though an internal company investigation had made public that the sexual harassment claims made against them were true. One claim that the company investigated came from former employee Loretta Lee. Lee had filed a lawsuit against Google for discrimination, retaliation, and wrongful termination. She claimed that she was subjected to constant harassment due to a culture that rewards macho men whose toxic behavior prioritizes winning above respect for others. In response to this and the *New York Times* report, on November 1, 2018, nearly twenty thousand Google employees had had enough. They went on strike and protested how the company handled sexual harassment allegations. These protesters demanded a right to bring a coworker with them to human resource meetings and to end forced arbitration for everyone. Arbitration is a method of resolving disputes outside of court, and when used for cases of sexual harassment, it typically results in the employees signing NDAs, thus forgoing their right to bring complaints to court. Google responded to these demands by making arbitration optional for individual cases of sexual harassment and sexual assault. The protest and Google's response to it then led to a series of protests throughout many companies based in Silicon Valley.

In response to the Uber and Google sexual misconduct scandals, many companies within the tech industry have been working hard to eliminate the toxic culture for women. For example, on November 9, 2018, Facebook ended its policy of forced arbitration against sexual harassment claims. Other companies, such as Microsoft, had eliminated their arbitration clauses even before Google's massive walkout. In late 2017, Microsoft announced that it would allow employees to sue the company for sexual harassment claims rather than forcing them into arbitration. Still, other companies have a ways to go. Amazon, for example, still requires its employees to sign away their rights to go to court to settle

Google employees stage a walkout in San Francisco in November 2018. They were protesting the company's sexual harassment policies and its actions in connection with allegations against company executives.

sexual harassment and discrimination disputes. And Amazon is not alone. Companies in a wide range of industries are also slowly moving toward meeting the demands made by the #MeToo Movement. One of these is the finance and banking industry.

The Financial Sector

Like businesses in most industries, financial firms have been forced to publicly confront allegations of sexual harassment. For example, Social Finance, Inc., an online lending firm, has been sued by a former employee who alleges that CEO Mike Cagney "fosters a sexually charged corporate culture that condones unlawful conduct."[30] Cagney responded by announcing that the company would conduct an internal investigation, but he later resigned as questions about his own conduct surfaced. Similarly, Fidelity Investments dismissed two different managers after each faced accusations of sexual harassment. The company's CEO, Abby Johnson, responded to these claims by saying, "We have no tolerance at our company for any type of harassment. We simply will not, and do not, tolerate this type of behavior, from anyone."[31]

As in the tech industry, women in the financial sector have known that they would risk their reputations by coming forward with allegations of workplace sexual misconduct. The pyramid-like power structure of companies within the finance industry includes many junior women at the bottom of the structure and fewer toward the top. Financial institutions are built on relationships that hinge on discretion, reputation, and sacrifice. In many firms, the workplace culture is so intimidating that women feel that shedding light on their sexual harassment stories could greatly damage their own careers, their boss's reputations, and their company.

In January 2018, Bloomberg News interviewed twenty women who used to work or still work on Wall Street. The women were not named in the article. All reported that they had seen some changes in their work environment since the advent of the #MeToo Movement. These changes included more intensive sexual harassment education and prevention seminars as well as changed attitudes by their coworkers. The writer noted that many of the women described similar experiences that spanned their careers. They described being grabbed, kissed out of the blue, humiliated, and propositioned by colleagues and bosses but remained quiet because of the cultural and financial forces that are particularly strong in banking.

> **"One major bank can inspire others in the financial sector to do the right thing."[32]**
>
> —Lift Our Voices

Two years after this Bloomberg report, one bank has finally stepped up to meet the changing demands issued by the #MeToo Movement. In February 2020 Wells Fargo became the first of the big banks to no longer require arbitration when employees file sexual harassment claims. In response to Wells Fargo's actions, the anti-NDA group Lift Our Voices said in a statement, "One major bank can inspire others in the financial sector to do the right thing."[32]

Across the Board

Changes since the #MeToo Movement can be seen in many areas of business. For example, so-called Weinstein clauses—referring to disclosure of any allegations of sexual harassment—are now included in many mergers and acquisitions. (These are transactions in which the ownership of a company and its assets is transferred to other entities.) Many of the changes that can be seen within companies are the firms' responses to meet new legal requirements. These legal requirements were implemented by the government in attempts to end workplace sexual harassment.

But in other cases, like Microsoft and Wells Fargo, companies are taking it upon themselves to act proactively in the wake of #MeToo. This is not only because these companies' employees are pushing toward healthier work environments but also because employees have more outside resources to help them when confronted with workplace sexual misconduct. Organizations like Time's Up are working tirelessly to assist women from every industry to combat the sexual harassment they face in their careers.

Ripples in Education

Most of the discussion raised by the #MeToo Movement has focused on sexual harassment in the workplace. The topic of sexual harassment has also filtered into other areas of daily life, including education. The biggest ripples have been felt at the college and university level, but sexual harassment is also being discussed in many of the nation's elementary and secondary schools.

#MeToo Knows No Age

Difficult as it may be to believe, experts say that sexual harassment is an issue for schools teaching kindergarten through twelfth grade (K–12). "First and foremost, sexual harassment is occurring at the K–12 level,"[33] says Anne Hedgepeth, the interim vice president of public policy and government relations for the American Association of University Women (AAUW). Prior to #MeToo, this problem was largely hidden from public view because most incidents were not reported. Research on sexual harassment in the nation's elementary and secondary schools has been limited and contradictory. However, one AAUW study found that nearly half of students in grades seven through twelve (and more than half of female students) said they had experienced sexual harassment at school. Most of these incidents were never officially reported, however.

Since the #MeToo Movement, this has been changing. From students' active use of social media and witnessing the increased focus on accountability, young people are beginning to feel more comfortable reporting experiences of sexual misconduct. This is largely because there are now many influential role models who are saying that is okay to speak up (and schools are taking these reports more seriously). When actress Laura Dern gave her acceptance speech at the 2018 Golden Globes, for instance, she said, "May we teach our children that speaking out without the fear of retribution is our culture's new North Star."[34]

> **"May we teach our children that speaking out without the fear of retribution is our culture's new North Star."[34]**
>
> —Laura Dern, actress

Encouraging students to speak up about sexual harassment is the goal of Stop Sexual Assault in Schools (SSAIS), a national nonprofit organization that launched the hashtag *#MeTooK12* (pronounced "Me Too K–12") in 2017. The goal was to bolster attention in an area that had received much less public notice. "Few people of influence understand how sexual harassment and assault devastate the lives of K–12 students, their families, and friends—beginning in elementary school;

Studies show that sexual harassment occurs in K–12 schools, with both male and female students as the victims, but has been largely hidden from public view. This is changing thanks to the #MeToo Movement.

and the younger the victim, the more devastating the impact and greater vulnerability to repeated assault,"[35] SSAIS explained in a 2018 announcement. #MeTooK12 seeks to send a powerful message: that sexual assault and harassment have no age limit and that young people who experience these issues firsthand are not alone.

One of the biggest problems for teens is not knowing what constitutes sexual consent and not understanding the difference between healthy and unhealthy relationship habits. This is the finding of a 2018 study of public schools by the Center for American Progress. Only 16 percent of American public schools teach healthy relationship habits through their sex education programs, the study found. Moreover, only twenty-four states and the District of Columbia even require sex education in public schools. Out of these twenty-four, only California, Hawaii, New Jersey, North Carolina, Oregon, Rhode Island, Vermont, and West Virginia require the topic of consent to be included in the school's curriculum. "States are not providing students with enough guidance and support in terms of how to behave in the world they grew up in," said the Center for American Progress's Catherine Brown. "It's really important to be clear with them about what is and what isn't permissible and what the lines are when dealing with other people in relationships."[36] Once students begin attending college, however, the topic of consent is one of the biggest keywords students hear on campus because it is a requirement by federal law that universities teach it.

"States are not providing students with enough guidance and support in terms of how to behave in the world they grew up in."[36]

—Catherine Brown, Center for American Progress

Teaching Consent

In the #MeToo age, the topic of consent has gained new importance—especially on college campuses. Consent refers to an agreement between individuals to engage in sexual activity.

It Is Never Too Early to Teach Consent

In a CBS News interview, Monica Rivera, the director of the Women and Gender Advocacy Center at Colorado State University offered her thoughts on how to teach consent to kids:

> I think that we often make the mistake of not treating the topic of consent the way we treat other elements of . . . what we teach kids. . . . I think that we really need to be shifting how we talk about consent . . . so that we're teaching age-appropriate topics of consent from kindergarten all the way through twelfth grade.
>
> Obviously . . . we're not going to be teaching kindergartners about sex, but there are ways that we can be teaching them about concepts of body sovereignty, and about respecting each other's bodies and what it means to have body autonomy at as early of an age as possible. . . .
>
> I would never just walk over and drink out of somebody's water bottle or grab a pen out of someone's hand. . . . What we need to be able to do is set that foundation as it relates to bodies. . . . What [asking for consent] looks like is . . . asking "Hey would you like a hug?" But even more importantly, it's letting our kids see us say, "Hmm, no thanks, not today," and then say, "Okay, cool." [This way] we can model that it's really not a big deal to be rejected.

Quoted in CBS News, "Why It's Never Too Early to Teach Children About Consent," April 28, 2019. www.cbsnews.com.

There are many ways that it can be given, but the bottom line is that consent requires clear communication. Phrases like "Is this okay?" should be used when the type of sexual activity changes and should not continue until both parties have given their permission. Consent is also revocable. This means that if individuals have given their permission to engage in some form of sexual activity, and then later express that they are uncomfortable and want to stop, their wishes are to be respected. Consent is often defined as revocable, enthusiastic, conscious, verbal, ongoing, and sober.

The problem is that, in practice, consent is not always clear-cut. Despite efforts to teach young people that yes means yes and no means no, there is a fuzzy and complicated middle ground. It is often referred to as the gray zone.

There are various scenarios of what happens in the gray zone. Sometimes one person initiates, sometimes both do, and still other times it is difficult to tell. Sometimes one person wants to engage in some sexual activity, but not all of it. Maybe someone gives his or her consent in one instance but wants to revoke that consent once the act goes further. Additionally, when alcohol is introduced, these scenarios can become even fuzzier. The complicated nature of consent has led colleges and universities to try different methods in educating their students on how to navigate the topic's murky waters.

"People often ask, 'Why teach consent?'" says sociologist Harry Brod, a professor at the University of Northern Iowa. To this he replies, "Because we often have entirely different understandings of what it means."[37] A recent study revealed that 61 percent of men say they rely on their partner's nonverbal cues, like body language, to indicate sexual consent. However, only 10 percent of women reported actually giving consent through body language; the majority wait to be asked. The #MeToo Movement has put the spotlight on the ambiguous nature of consent and has demanded that society clarifies its definition. Today consent is still a complicated topic, but the discrepancies, different understandings, and problems are being discussed more than ever before.

One change that began even before the rise of the #MeToo Movement is the idea that "yes means yes" should have more weight than "no means no." The assumption behind this is that by requiring a clear and affirmative answer, potential ambiguities would be eliminated. Students are taught to receive clear, continuous, and enthusiastic consent, rather than pursuing sexual activity until one party says no.

Today, in the wake of #MeToo, universities still use the "yes means yes" mantra, but they are also educating students about how to navigate through the gray zone. Some schools use a traffic light analogy. If the light is currently yellow, individuals must have

The topic of consent has gained new importance in the #MeToo age. Many colleges and universities are teaching students what constitutes consent, or clear communication, in the context of sexual activity.

a green light before continuing. This means that if they are unsure about the other person's consent, they must become sure before they go further. Other programs begin with a YouTube video that compares consent to tea. The video explains, "If you say 'Hey, would you like a cup of tea?' and they're like, 'Uh, you know, I'm not really sure,' then you can make them a cup of tea, or not, but be aware they might not drink it. And if they don't drink it—and this is the important part—then don't make them drink it."[38]

Confusing Cultural Cues

But consent is also made vague by culture. Although this is an era when women are empowered to say yes to sex, they are also confronted by oversexualized characters in movies and magazines who imply that, to be desirable, they also must be coy in their flirtations and timid in their consent. Moreover, "They've been socialized to think that 'yes' means you're a slut, 'maybe' means you're a tease, and 'no' means you're a prude,"[39] writes Jessica Bennett, the gender editor for the *New York Times*. Culture also clouds men's point of view. In movies and television, when a woman says "no" to a man's sexual advances, it is often portrayed as a flirtatious and bashful ploy aimed at making the man try harder. On-screen, "no" is negotiable. "A lot of what we as young men learn as seduction is really more like preparatory sexual assault training,"[40] said Brod. Sexual consent is the most valued it has ever been, but understanding it is also more complicated than ever before. The #MeToo Movement has opened the door on discuss-

Mixed cultural messages can create confusion. Women have the power of consent but oversexualized characters in movies and magazines can muddy the meaning of "no" and "yes."

ing these complexities while simultaneously stressing its importance on the national level.

> "They've been socialized to think that 'yes' means you're a slut, 'maybe' means you're a tease, and 'no' means you're a prude."[39]
>
> —Jessica Bennett, gender editor for the *New York Times*

Since #MeToo began, college campuses all across the country have ramped up training seminars and sex education training. They now include education on supporting friends when they have experienced sexual misconduct and how to not be a bystander when someone witnesses sexual harassment or assault. All universities extensively educate their students on how to drink alcohol responsibly. In the wake of #MeToo, these education initiatives have been expanded to include discussions of recognizing, preventing, and reporting sexual violence. Most colleges now require all new employees and students to take a sexual violence and harassment prevention training seminar prior to working at or attending the school. These seminars also teach students how to drink alcohol responsibly. In addition, they provide contact information for school therapists, crisis hotlines, and support groups.

Have Colleges Gone Too Far?

Many argue that colleges and universities seem to be leading the way in the new culture of #MeToo, but others contend that some of them have gone too far. These concerns relate specifically to punitive measures taken against those accused of sexual misconduct. This view stems in part from 2011, when the Obama administration began requiring colleges to encourage students to report unwelcome sexual advances and situations where they felt pressured to grant sexual favors. The policy implied that even before any verdicts were made against the accused, the university could take interim measures. These measures can include removing the accused students from certain classes, limiting their movements on campus, and sometimes banning them from school.

The #MeToo Movement has empowered female college students to report unwanted advances and sexual misconduct by fellow students. As a result, there are more instances of interim measures being taken even before any fact-finding has occurred. This is a concern not just for those students but also for some faculty, who contend that the pendulum may have swung too far in the opposite direction. There was a time when women who complained about sexual misconduct were viewed with suspicion and were often not believed. This has largely changed, but now "some colleges and universities fail even to give students the complaint against them, or notice of the factual basis of the charges, the evidence gathered, or the identities of witnesses,"[41] wrote Harvard Law School professor Elizabeth Bartholet and her colleagues in a 2017 paper.

This, they contend, is a different problem but a problem nevertheless. For example, in 2015 a California judge ordered the University of California, San Diego, to reverse the suspension of a male student who was accused of sexual assault. The judge ruled that university officials denied the student his due process rights during a hearing they conducted on the allegations made against him. The student had sued the university, contending that it violated his due process rights by presuming guilt ahead of his hearing, not allowing him access to witnesses and evidence, and informing a hearing panel of his guilt instead of letting the panel reach its own conclusion. This case, one of the first of its kind, has been seen as a road map for others who feel they have been unfairly punished as a result of sexual misconduct allegations.

In many of these cases, the plaintiffs have received positive responses from judges who are shocked at some of the policies colleges have implemented. The National Center for Higher Education Risk Management has even warned "that unless campus processes were reformed, a backlash could set back the entire consent movement."[42]

A Lack of Due Process

In a 2017 paper titled "Fairness for All Students Under Title IX," four Harvard Law School professors addressed their concerns about the lack of due process in how some universities deal with sexual misconduct allegations:

> "Though [the Office of Civil Rights] did not require schools to treat accused students unfairly in the investigation and adjudication process, its tactics put pressure on them to stack the system so as to favor alleged victims over those they accuse. The procedures for enforcing these definitions are frequently so unfair as to be truly shocking. Some colleges and universities fail even to give students the complaint against them, or notice of the factual basis of charges, the evidence gathered, or the identities of witnesses. Some schools fail to provide hearings or to allow the accused student's lawyer to attend or speak at hearings. Some bar the accused from putting questions to the accuser or witnesses, even through intermediaries. Some schools hold hearings in which the accuser participates while remaining unseen behind a partition. Some schools deny parties the right to see the investigative report or get copies for their lawyers for preparing an appeal. Some schools allow appeals only on very narrow grounds such as new evidence or procedural error, providing no meaningful check on the initial decisionmaker."

Quoted in Elizabeth Bartholet et al., "Fairness for All Students Under Title IX," Digital Access to Scholarship at Harvard, Harvard Library, Office of Scholarly Communication, August 21, 2017. https://dash.harvard.edu.

Change Is in the Air

All levels of educational institutions are feeling the changes brought about by #MeToo. Secondary schools are adopting more programs that teach consent and healthy relationships because of how pervasive sexual misconduct has been on college campuses for decades. To combat this, universities have long been on the cutting edge of the consent movement and the implementation of practices aimed at ending sexual misconduct. The #MeToo Movement has brought to light that perhaps a primary reason why universities have such a persistent issue with sexual harassment and assault is because their incoming students have not yet been educated on consent and how it relates to alcohol. Although consent at college has been a longtime initiative, many campuses have recently come under fire for taking sexual misconduct prevention measures too far. The accused's right to due process cannot be denied. But in the age of believing women and #MeToo, many feel that universities are improperly handling sexual misconduct cases by not giving a fair hearing to the accused. A balance between protecting survivors and respecting the accused has yet to be achieved, but the #MeToo Movement has opened up this discussion and change is in the air.

Toward an Uncertain Future

The #MeToo Movement has changed the way the world values accountability. The original aim of #MeToo, portraying the magnitude of sexual misconduct against women and creating solidarity among survivors, has been achieved. "Any person who takes issue with #MeToo is taking issue, first and foremost, with people saying, yes, this happened to me, too,"[43] says author Mark Greene. Nonetheless, there is another side of this change and progression, and that is uncertainty. Many are hesitant about how to navigate the workplace. Many people, especially men, are unsure what exactly constitutes sexual harassment. Some people, mostly men, have become fearful of being falsely accused of it. This fear has led to some unintended consequences.

> **"Any person who takes issue with #MeToo is taking issue, first and foremost, with people saying, yes, this happened to me, too."[43]**
>
> —Mark Greene, author

Definition and Perception

Part of the problem stems from the definition of sexual harassment that has been enshrined in law. That definition was adopted in 1980 when the US Equal Employment Opportunity Commission (EEOC) made sexual harassment a form of sex discrimination prohibited by the 1964 Civil Rights Act. The EEOC defines sexual harassment in an online publication titled, "Facts About Sexual Harassment." It reads,

Unwelcome sexual advances, requests for sexual favors, and other verbal or physical conduct of a sexual nature constitutes sexual harassment when submission to or rejection of this conduct explicitly or implicitly affects an individual's employment, unreasonably interferes with an individual's work performance or creates an intimidating, hostile or offensive work environment.[44]

The EEOC definition did not include an explicit list of what constitutes sexual harassment. This was intentional because interpretations and perceptions of sexual harassment differ from one

A Clearer Understanding

The #MeToo Movement and Time's Up, the organization founded by Hollywood celebrities, have influenced younger generations more than older generations. Polling results released by CBS News in 2020 show that 40 percent of men and women between the ages of eighteen and twenty-nine believe their understanding of sexual misconduct has been made clearer by the efforts of these two groups. In contrast, fewer than one-third of individuals in each of two categories of older adults say these groups have clarified their understanding of sexual misconduct.

Views of Sexual Misconduct: Made Clearer Because of #MeToo and Time's Up (by Age)

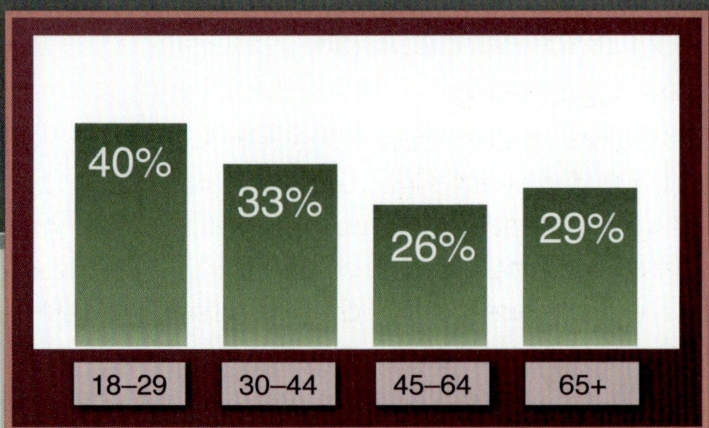

Source: Fred Backus and Jennifer de Pinto, "#MeToo and Time's Up: Most Think the Movements Are Making Progress—CBS News Poll," CBS News, January 7, 2020. www.cbsnews.com.

person to the next. As a result, there is lots of room for confusion about the definition and its application in the real world.

The act of hugging or placing a hand on a coworker's shoulder offers an example of the confusion that exists today. One person may think it is a friendly or supportive gesture, but another person may view the act as intimidating or as an unwanted sexual advance. It is unlikely that women in the late twentieth century would have reported these sorts of actions as sexual harassment even if they felt threatened. That is less true today. However, it is also true that some women will consider these types of actions to be harassment—and some will not. Circumstances and perceptions vary, which is part of what makes this new worldview confusing.

There is also now an underlying sense of fear that one may possibly be held accountable for an action that, up until the last few years, had genuinely seemed innocent and perfectly acceptable. According to a Pew Research Center poll, 66 percent of men over age sixty believe that in the wake of the #MeToo Movement, it is now more difficult to navigate workplace interactions. It can be hard to rapidly learn the nuances of cultural shifts, especially when the consequences for not adapting quickly enough can destroy a person's career or even his life. Additionally, there is now a growing fear of facing consequences for actions that were not intended to be harmful or might not have even taken place. This is because in this new era, accusations made against someone are supposed to be initially believed instead of assumed as false or as an overreaction on the part of the accuser.

False Accusations

False accusations, though few, have received widespread media attention in the years since #MeToo and #BelieveWomen. The hashtag *#BelieveWomen* arose out of the #MeToo Movement because in decades and years prior, sexual misconduct allegations were often disregarded as falsehoods. Men were believed far more often than women. The message behind both #MeToo and #BelieveWomen is that when victims speak up, they are to be believed. However, the United States was founded on the premise that individuals are innocent until proven guilty, and not the other way around. *Due process* traditionally refers to a fair course of action taken by the legal system, but in the context of sexual misconduct allegations, there are broader implications. Whereas alleged sexual misconduct victims are granted anonymity, whether it be in the courts, workplace, or universities, the defendants are publicly named. Even before a fair investigation is launched, many defendants' reputations are tarnished, which may result in the loss of their jobs, friends, and family. For this reason, a new culture of fear has surfaced in navigating workplace interactions. A survey released by the *Hollywood Reporter* in January 2019 revealed that "false accusations of sexual harassment was the number one gender issue men were concerned about, rated higher than actual harassment or equal pay."[45]

The easy relations between workers of the opposite sex, as shown in this photo, have gotten more difficult due to confusion, especially among men, about what constitutes harassment.

Though the #MeToo Movement's intent was to focus on accountability and believing women, many have received a different message. "Their biggest takeaway from #MeToo was not that powerful men have been harassing women with impunity for decades but rather that conniving women are inventing stories to deliberately take down men's careers,"[46] writes *Washington Post* columnist Monica Hesse. The fear of false accusations in the era of empowered women is real, though statistically unfounded. Studies have recorded that the number of false sexual assault allegations compose only 2 to 8 percent of total allegations.

Unintended Consequences

Although the majority of businesses are taking steps to strengthen sexual harassment policies, some individuals are navigating through this new and unfamiliar terrain in ways that have negative results for female workers. One of the most extreme cases has come to be known as the "Pence rule." This stems from Vice President Mike Pence's statement that by never dining or having drinks alone with a woman other than his wife, he avoids any appearance, and thus allegations, of indecency. In a 2018 Bloomberg article, many businessmen who were interviewed reported "how uneasy they are about being alone with female colleagues, particularly youthful and attractive ones, fearful of the rumor mill or of, as one put it, the potential liability."[47]

This type of concern is also borne out by polling. A 2018 Pew Research Center survey has revealed that "51 percent of Americans believe the increased focus on sexual harassment and assault has made it more difficult for men to know how to interact with women at work."[48] To avoid the risk of running afoul of new attitudes or making their female coworkers uncomfortable, some of the male respondents to the survey say they have constructed personal rules for themselves. These include not meeting with women in rooms without windows, keeping one's distance in elevators, no business dinners with women under age thirty-five, no business trips with women, and keeping the door open during private business meetings. These types of measures can have damaging consequences for professional women, who may be excluded from important business trips or from networking with male colleagues.

Even more damaging, recent reports have indicated a growing reluctance by men in positions of authority to work closely with or even hire women. "It's not a good thing," said Kellie McElhaney, the founding director of the Center for Equity, Gender, and Leadership at the Haas School of Business of the University of California, Berkeley. "It's further disconnecting women from networks that we've already been excluded from. There are solutions, but I think right now men are a bit paralyzed."[49]

This new culture of uncertainty in the wake of #MeToo is not limited to workplace interactions. Men are being asked to change the ways in which they interact with women in other settings as well. They are also being required to reshape how they identify as men in society and how they teach younger generations about respect and accountability. This task has become quite confusing for some, especially as new labels like *toxic masculinity* have become common vocabulary. This term has arisen in the wake of #MeToo because many of the behaviors that lead to sexual misconduct stem from men's ideas of what exactly it is that makes them a man.

> **"It's further disconnecting women from networks that we've already been excluded from. There are solutions, but I think right now men are a bit paralyzed."[49]**
>
> —Kellie McElhaney, Center for Equity, Gender and Leadership

Role Models and Toxic Masculinity

In this era of empowered women, female politicians, and feminist celebrities, women and girls are presented with a plethora of role models and inspiring idols. On the other hand, men and boys

Hope for the Future

Jessica Bennett became the gender editor for the *New York Times* in November 2017 and has rigorously been covering the #MeToo Movement and gender equality since. Now she has a few wishes for the years to come:

> I hope we can shift public focus away from celebrities like Ashley Judd who were abused by celebrities like Harvey Weinstein to women like Suzette Wright, who suffered in silence for years at Ford Motor Co., and the thousands of women who face sexual harassment daily but may not have the means or access to pursue legal cases or media articles. . . .
>
> I hope we begin to see men and women step up as bystanders, one of the few ways proven effective at combatting workplace harassment and discrimination. . . .
>
> I hope we talk about *culture* as much as we talk about individuals, and recognize that while the Weinsteins of the world are extreme, the messages we learn about sex, and power, and courtship, and consent, are deeply ingrained and start young—and will take far more than a workplace sexual harassment training to unlearn.
>
> I hope we can have meaningful, nuanced discussions about due process and women's agency. What can someone accused of sexual misconduct reasonably expect, what is fair, and what range of punishments should be considered beyond the abrupt torching of someone's career?

Quoted in Jessica Bennett, "The #MeToo Moment: What's Next?," *New York Times*, January 5, 2018. www.nytimes.com.

are learning how they fit into a society that is drastically different from the culture of their fathers and grandfathers. They are having to navigate the uncharted territory of redefining masculinity in ways that mesh with new and evolving social standards. A 2017 study of men ages eighteen to thirty in the United States, Mexico, and the United Kingdom by gender justice organization Promundo and Unilever found that almost all respondents felt pressured to conform to traditional societal expectations of masculinity. Researchers have defined traditional masculinity as a set of behaviors and beliefs that encompass seven pillars: being self-sufficient without asking for help, acting tough even if they feel scared, looking physically attractive, adhering to rigid masculine gender roles, being heterosexual, having as many sexual partners as they can, and exerting aggression and control. These norms have recently been dubbed *toxic masculinity*. This does not mean that masculinity is toxic; rather, it refers to "what can come of teaching boys that they can't express emotion openly; that they have to be 'tough all the time'; that anything other than that makes them 'feminine' or weak,"[50] writes *New York Times* reporter Maya Salam.

Confronting toxic masculinity is a growing discussion on the national and international stage. The younger generation of men within the music industry have most noticeably been taking the first steps in redefining masculinity. Musicians from around the world are gaining widespread audiences by artistically attacking what some consider to be the stifling framework of what it means to be a man. In 2018 the British band Idles released *Joy as an Act of Resistance*, an album that uses toxic masculinity as a primary theme. The English neo-emo band As It Is began to strip down this notion of masculinity in June 2019 by releasing the single "The Stigma (Boys Don't Cry)," which has been streamed over 13 million times on Spotify. Many other artists, including Tiny Moving Parts, Henry Jamison, and Sam Fender, have released music that confronts societal expectations of men. Each of these artists say that their music is a direct result of the #MeToo Movement. "All these norms that we see aren't normal at all," says Joe Talbot, the lead singer and writer for Idles. "It's a giant lie."[51]

A Global Future

Redefining masculinity on the international stage mirrors how the #MeToo Movement has spread globally. The hashtag has been translated into dozens of languages and has gone viral across the

> **"All these norms that we see aren't normal at all. It's a giant lie."[51]**
>
> —Joe Talbot, lead singer and writer for Idles

The #MeToo Movement has spread far beyond US borders. In 2018 these protesters took to the streets in Seoul, South Korea, where sexual harassment is common but gets little attention.

globe. As in the United States, the impacts of this global trend can be seen with changes in law, precedents set by the courts, and changed norms in business.

The South Korean version of the #MeToo Movement originated in January 2018 during a televised interview when a female prosecutor publicly accused her former boss of sexual misconduct. According to a South Korean news reporter, "The [#MeToo] movement was relatively quiet in the socially conservative South Korea—that was until female prosecutor Seo Ji-hyeon came forward with her own story of sexual harassment. The prosecutor's revelation appears to have sparked a movement in Korea, where sexual harassment in the workplace is prevalent but often ignored."[52] Seo Ji-hyeon's decision to make her allegations public was completely unprecedented; in South Korea, survivors of sexual violence have been afraid to speak up out of shame and fear of retaliation. But, after the interview aired, hundreds of other women came forward with their own stories

Detoxifying Masculinity

In a 2017 opinion article for *The Guardian*, hip-hop artist Jordan Stephens discussed his belief that it is the responsibility of men to confront toxic masculinity and gain emotional intelligence:

> Any man who has read a woman's account of harassment or assault and thought "that doesn't apply to me": what you're experiencing in that moment is the exact privilege, power and entitlement that women are finding space to battle against.
>
> . . .
>
> I believe that the false power gifted to me as a man in our society didn't allow me the space to understand, cry, and work through the pain of my past and duality of my present. This idea that male vulnerability is undesirable—it covers up the pain of so many troubled boys who wanted more hugs from their mum or have missed the company of their dad, or were victims of abuse or loneliness or just generally felt as though they had no time, space, company or even the words to describe how they felt.
>
> It's our responsibility as we become adults to acknowledge this pain and gain compassion for ourselves and acceptance of others. . . .
>
> It's OK to feel sad. It's OK to cry. . . . It's OK to have . . . wanted more affection. It's OK to take a moment when you're reminded of these truths.

Jordan Stephens, "Toxic Masculinity Is Everywhere. It's Up to Us Men to Fix This," *The Guardian*, October 23, 2017. www.theguardian.com.

of sexual harassment. As in the United States, these stories led to the resignation of several prominent figures in the sports and music industries as well as some of the country's top politicians.

Many other countries are seeing changes in their legal precedents and social norms. For example, in August 2017 in Egypt, security camera footage captured Rania Fahmy, a young woman, using her handbag to fight back against an attacker. This footage went viral and ignited not only a regional conversation regarding sexual assault but also an entirely new legal precedent for Egyptian women. Using the video as evidence, Fahmy filed charges against her attacker and became the first woman in Egypt to win a court ruling on sexual assault charges. Egypt is not alone in experiencing changes like this. In France, the minister for gender equality, Marlène Schiappa responded to the demands of the #MeToo Movement by proposing a bill that extends the statute of limitations for sex crimes and creates new sanctions for cyberstalking, street harassment, and catcalling. The bill was enacted into law in 2018.

The #MeToo Movement continues to make progress toward women's rights all across the world. In Spain, after a wave of protests in April 2018 over light sentences for convicted rapists, the Spanish government promised to strengthen the laws against rape. One of the landmark developments that played out on the global stage is the minimum obligations standards created by the International Labour Organization (ILO) in June 2019. These new international legal standards regarding sexual violence and harassment at work have the potential to alter sexual harassment laws around the world. "Governments should ratify and carry out the new ILO Violence and Harassment convention as soon as possible," says Nisha Varia, the women's rights advocacy director at Human Rights Watch. "The #MeToo movement has exposed deeply entrenched norms that enable abuse, and urgent action is needed to ensure that all workers are guaranteed their safety and dignity."[53] The #MeToo Movement has circled around the world at the highest levels of government and has weaved its way, in some form or another, through all levels of daily life.

"The #MeToo movement has exposed deeply entrenched norms that enable abuse, and urgent action is needed to ensure that all workers are guaranteed their safety and dignity."[53]

—Nisha Varia, Human Rights Watch

Going Forward: Healing Trauma

The changes that have come from the #MeToo Movement, have been positive for some while negative for others. For many, the movement has created an underlying sense of female empowerment and has motivated women to speak up about their experiences of sexual misconduct. For others, it has manifested in fear and uncertainty about how to navigate through unfamiliar waters. And for a few, #MeToo has sparked flashbacks and has reopened old wounds.

Tarana Burke wants people to remember that the original motivation for the movement was to help survivors recover from trauma. What she wants to reinforce is that the core of the movement is about healing and connecting survivors to proper resources. She says, "We don't believe in collecting stories of people's trauma. . . . We believe in sharing peoples' stories of healing. When you start talking about what you've done to cope and how you have developed practices around healing, that's something that people need to see."[54]

Introduction: Breaking the Silence

1. Quoted in Gretchen Carlson, "Gretchen Carlson: Fox News, I Want My Voice Back," *New York Times*, December 12, 2019. www.nytimes.com.
2. Quoted in James Crowley, "Ex Fox News Hosts Who Called Out Sexual Harassment Begin 'Lift Our Voices' to Stop NDA Coverups," *Newsweek*, December 10, 2019. www.newsweek.com.

Chapter One: Solidarity, Awareness, and Accountability

3. Quoted in Brent Lang, "How *New York Times* Reporters Broke Hollywood's Biggest Sexual Harassment Story," *Variety*, December 13, 2017. www.variety.com.
4. Quoted in Nadja Sayej, "Alyssa Milano on the #MeToo Movement: 'We're Not Going to Stand for It Any More,'" *The Guardian* (Manchester, UK), December 1, 2017. www.theguardian com.
5. Quoted in Sayej, "Alyssa Milano on the #MeToo Movement."
6. Quoted in Tarana Burke, "Me Too Is a Movement, Not a Moment," TEDWomen 2018. www.ted.com.
7. Quoted in Chris Snyder and Linette Lopez, "Tarana Burke on Why She Created the #MeToo Movement—and Where It's Headed," Business Insider, December 13, 2017. www.businessinsider.com.
8. Quoted in Stephanie Zacharek, Eliana Dockterman, and Haley Sweetland Edwards, "*Time* Person of the Year: The Silence Breakers," *Time*, December 6, 2017. https://time.com.
9. Quoted in Mary Pflum, "A Year Ago, Alyssa Milano Started a Conversation About #MeToo. These Women Replied," NBC News, October 15, 2018. www.nbcnews.com.
10. Quoted in Pflum, "A Year Ago, Alyssa Milano Started a Conversation About #MeToo."
11. Quoted in Pflum, "A Year Ago, Alyssa Milano Started a Conversation About #MeToo."

12. Quoted in *Time*, "'Our Pain Is Never Prioritized.' #MeToo Founder Tarana Burke Says We Must Listen to 'Untold' Stories of Minority Women," April 23, 2019. https://time.com.
13. Quoted in Rochelle Riley, "MeToo Founder Tarana Burke Blasts the Movement for Ignoring Poor Women," *Detroit Free Press*, November 15, 2018. www.freep.com.
14. Quoted in Zacharek, Dockterman, and Edwards, "*Time* Person of the Year."
15. Quoted in Zacharek, Dockterman, and Edwards, "*Time* Person of the Year."
16. Quoted in Zacharek, Dockterman, and Edwards, "*Time* Person of the Year."

Chapter Two: An Altered Legal and Political Landscape

17. Quoted in Zoe Greenberg, "What Has Actually Changed in a Year," *New York Times*, October 6, 2018. www.nytimes.com.
18. Quoted in Sarah Lyall, "Abroad in America: What Is Firing Up Female Candidates?," *New York Times*, October 26, 2018. www.nytimes.com.
19. Quoted in Charlette Alter, "A Year Ago, They Marched. Now a Record Number of Women Are Running for Office," *Time*, January 18, 2018. https://time.com.
20. Quoted in Ally Boguhn, "The Personal Is Political for Women Running for Office in the #MeToo Era," Rewire News, July 24, 2018. www.rewirenews.com.
21. Quoted in Emily Shugerman, "The #MeToo Movement Takes Office After Winning Elections Across the US," Daily Beast, November 7, 2018. www.thedailybeast.com.
22. Quoted in *New York Times*, "Brett Kavanaugh's Opening Statement: Full Transcript," September 26, 2018. www.nytimes.com.

Chapter Three: The Business World Adapts

23. Quoted in Hector Tobar, "The Time's Up Initiative Built upon the Work Done by These Labor Activists," *Smithsonian*, December 2018. www.smithsonianmag.com.

24. Quoted in Time's Up, "Companies Can Lead the Way on Gender Equality." www.timesupnow.org.
25. Quoted in Olivia Truffaut-Wong, "9 Ways 'Me Too' Has Already Impacted Movies, from Inclusion Riders to 'Wonder Woman 2,'" Bustle, March 21, 2018. www.bustle.com.
26. Quoted in Andrea Mandell, "New Survey Casts a Wide Net to Quantify Hollywood Harassment Culture After #MeToo," *USA Today*, November 20, 2019. www.usatoday.com.
27. Quoted in Erica Gonzales, "Women Open Up About Wearing Black on the Golden Globes Red Carpet," *Harper's Bazaar*, January 7, 2018. www.harpersbazaar.com.
28. Quoted in Gonzales, "Women Open Up About Wearing Black on the Golden Globe's Red Carpet."
29. Quoted in Mike Isaac, "Uber Founder Travis Kalanick Resigns as CEO," *New York Times*, June 21, 2017. www.nytimes.com.
30. Quoted in Nathaniel M. Glasser, "The Weinstein Effect: Me Too Allegations in the Financial Services Industry," *National Law Review*, November 29, 2017. www.natlawreview.com.
31. Quoted in Glasser, "The Weinstein Effect."
32. Quoted in Daniel Taub and Hannah Levitt, "Wells Fargo Ends Forced Arbitration for Sexual Harassment," BloombergQuint, February 13, 2020. www.bloombergquint.com.

Chapter Four: Ripples in Education

33. Quoted in Lauren Camera, "#MeToo Goes To School," *US News*, January 8, 2018. www.usnews.com.
34. Quoted in Lauren Alexis Fisher, "Laura Dern Delivers Powerful Golden Globes Speech," *Harper's Bazaar*, January 7, 2018. www.harpersbazaar.com.
35. Quoted in Brittney McNamara, "People on Social Media Are Already Spreading the Message," *TeenVogue*, January 3, 2018. www.teenvogue.com.
36. Quoted in Christina Maxouris and Saeed Ahmed, "Only These 8 States Require Sex Education Classes to Mention Consent," CNN Health, September 29, 2018. www.cnn.com.
37. Quoted in Jessica Bennett, "Campus Sex . . . with a Syllabus," *New York Times*, January 9, 2016. www.nytimes.com.

38. Blue Seat Studios, "Tea Consent," YouTube, May 12, 2015. www.youtube.com.
39. Quoted in Bennett, "Campus Sex . . . with a Syllabus."
40. Quoted in Jessica Bennett, "When Saying 'Yes' Is Easier than Saying 'No,'" *New York Times*, December 16, 2017. www.nytimes.com.
41. Quoted in Elizabeth Bartholet et al., "Fairness for All Students Under Title IX," Digital Access to Scholarship at Harvard, Harvard Library, Office of Scholarly Communication, August 21, 2017. https://dash.harvard.edu.
42. Quoted in Emily Yoffe, "Why the #MeToo Movement Should Be Ready for a Backlash," *Politico*, December 10, 2017. www.politco.com.

Chapter Five: Toward an Uncertain Future

43. Quoted in Kaley Roshitsh, "'Manning Up' in the Wake of the #MeToo Movement," *Women's Wear Daily*, January 3, 2019. www.wwd.com.
44. US Equal Employment Opportunity Commission, "Facts About Sexual Harassment." www.eeoc.gov.
45. Quoted in Mia Brett, "Many in Media Distort the Framing of #MeToo," Women's Media Center, July 24, 2019. www.womensmediacenter.com.
46. Quoted in Monica Hesse, "For Robert Foster's Defenders, Men Are Victims and #MeToo Is the Real Villain," *Washington Post*, July 16, 2019. www.washingtonpost.com.
47. Gillian Tan and Katia Porzecanski, "Wall Street Rule for the #MeToo Era: Avoid Women at All Cost," Bloomberg, December 18, 2018, www.bloomberg.com.
48. Quoted in Jorge L. Ortiz, "Will #MeToo Turn into #NotHer? Movement May Come with Unintended Workplace Consequences," *USA Today*, October 4, 2018. www.usatoday.com.
49. Quoted in Ortiz, "Will #MeToo Turn into #NotHer?"
50. Quoted in Maya Salam, "What Is Toxic Masculinity?," *New York Times*, January 22, 2019. www.nytimes.com.
51. Quoted in Jim Farber, "The New Angry Young Men: Rockers Who Rail Against 'Toxic Masculinity,'" *New York Times*, January 11, 2019. www.nytimes.com.

52. Quoted in Meighan Stone and Rachel Vogelstein, "International Women's Day: Celebrating #MeToo's Global Impact," *Foreign Policy*, March 7, 2019. www.foreignpolicy.com.
53. Quoted in Human Rights Watch, "#MeToo Movement's Second Anniversary," October 14, 2019. www.hrw.org.
54. Quoted in Aisha Harris, "She Founded Me Too. Now She Wants to Move Past the Trauma," *New York Times*, October 15, 2018. www.nytimes.com.

A Call to Men—www.acalltomen.org

A Call to Men works with males of all ages to promote respectful behaviors and reduce the incidence of sexual harassment and other types of sexual misconduct. The website provides numerous educational materials as well as a link to the organization's blog, *Out of the Man Box*.

American Civil Liberties Union (ACLU)—www.aclu.org

The ACLU advocates for civil liberties and defends people whose rights are threatened. Its website focuses on issues and rights and provides links to a number of publications about sex discrimination.

Girls for Gender Equity—www.ggenyc.org

This organization supports the physical, psychological, social, and economic well-being of females of all ages, with a special focus on girls and women of color. The website offers a good collection of information about sexual harassment and other types of sexual misconduct.

Me Too—https://metoomvmt.org

This site, which is sponsored by the organization Girls for Gender Equity, offers a wealth of information about the #MeToo Movement. It features real-life stories, news articles, statistics, a searchable resource library, and a link to its blog.

Time's Up—www.timesupnow.com

Time's Up focuses on helping victims of sexual harassment with legal assistance and on advocating for stronger laws. The website offers a variety of resources, including articles about sexual harassment, news articles, frequently asked questions, and more.

US Equal Opportunity Employment Commission (EEOC)

www.eeoc.gov

The EEOC enforces federal antidiscrimination laws related to all aspects of employment. Numerous materials are available on its website, and its search engine produces a wealth of information on sex discrimination and related issues.

Books

Gretchen Carlson, *Be Fierce*. New York: Center Street, 2017.

Jim DeRogatis, *Soulless: The Case Against R. Kelly*. New York: Abrams, 2020.

Laurie Collier Hillstrom, *#MeToo Movement*. Santa Barbara, CA: ABC-CLIO, 2019.

Linda Hirshman, *Reckoning: The Epic Battle Against Sexual Abuse and Harassment*. Boston: Houghton Mifflin Harcourt, 2019.

Heather C. Hudak, *#MeToo Movement*. New York: Crabtree, 2019.

Jodi Kantor and Megan Twohey, *She Said: Breaking the Sexual Harassment Story That Helped Ignite a Movement*. New York: Penguin, 2019.

Peggy J. Parks, *The #MeToo Movement*. San Diego: Reference Point, 2020.

Mirande Valbrune, *#MeToo: A Practical Guide to Navigating Today's Cultural Workplace Revolution*. Miami: Employee Relate, 2018.

Internet Sources

Nanette Asimov, "#MeToo Movement Spurs #HimToo Backlash: 'People Don't Want to Believe,'" *San Francisco Chronicle*, October 13, 2018. www.sfchronicle.com.

Tarana Burke, "#MeToo Was Started for Black and Brown Women and Girls. They're Still Being Ignored," *Washington Post*, November 9, 2017. www.washingtonpost.com.

Alix Langone, "#MeToo and Time's Up Founders Explain the Difference Between the 2 Movements—and How They're Alike," *Time*, March 22, 2018. https://time.com.

Wendy Lu, “What #MeToo Means to Teenagers,” *New York Times*, April 19, 2018. www.nytimes.com.

Catharine MacKinnon, “Where #MeToo Came from and Where It’s Going,” *Atlantic*, March 2019. www.theatlantic.com.

Ayanna Runcie, “#MeToo for Youth: #GirlsToo Focuses on Teens’ Sexual Trauma,” CBS News, April 2, 2019. www.cbsnews.com.

Nancy Jo Sales, “MeToo in School: Too Many Children Are Sexually Harassed by Classmates,” Teen Kids News, September 20, 2018. https://teenkidsnews.com.

Nadia Sayej, “Alyssa Milano on the #MeToo Movement: ‘We’re Not Going to Stand for It Anymore,” *The Guardian*, December 1, 2017. www.theguardian.com.

Joanne N. Smith, “#MeToo Isn’t Just for Adults,” *Essence*, May 7, 2019. www.essence.com.

Kelly Wallace, “Will #MeToo Be a Turning Point for Younger Girls Too?,” CNN, January 1, 2018. www.cnn.com.

Stephanie Zacharek, Eliana Dockterman, and Haley Sweetland Edwards, “*Time* Person of the Year: The Silence Breakers,” *Time*, December 6, 2017. https://time.com.

Note: Boldface page numbers indicate illustrations.

Cover: sirtravelalot/Shutterstock.com

6: JStone/Shutterstock.com
9: Ga Fullner/Shutterstock.com
12: lev radin/Shutterstock.com
15: Sundry Photography/Shutterstock.com
21: fizkes/Shutterstock.com
23: lev radin/Shutterstock.com
27: Everett Collection/Newscom
32: Rightdx/iStock Photos
34: Tinseltown/Shutterstock.com
39: Associated Press
43: Monkey Business Images/Shutterstock.com
47: cdrin/Shutterstock.com
48: Halay Alex/Shutterstock.com
54: Maury Aaseng
56: Photographee.eu/Shutterstock.com
61: Socialtruant/Shutterstock.com

ABOUT THE AUTHOR

Brynn Reinkens is a recent graduate from the University of California, Berkeley. Having received her bachelor's degree in global studies with a minor in human rights, she is now living in San Diego as she continues to write in the years before attending law school.